CONTENTS

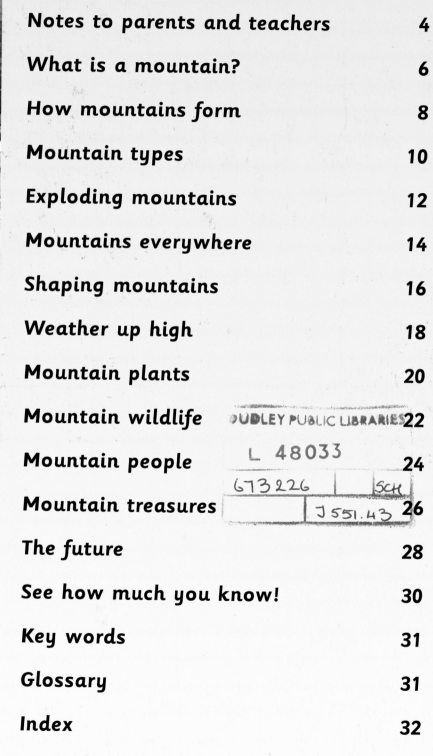

Notes to parents and teachers

This series has been developed for group use in the classroom as well as for children reading on their own. In particular, its differentiated text allows children of mixed abilities to enjoy reading about the same topic. The larger size text (A, below) offers apprentice readers a simplified text. This simplified text is used in the introduction to each chapter and in the picture captions. This font is part of the © Sassoon family of fonts recommended by the National Literacy Early Years Strategy document for maximum legibility. The smaller size text (B, below) offers a more challenging read for older or more able readers.

Exploding mountains

Sometimes mountains are formed when boiling runny rock bursts from the ground and hardens.

A

 Volcanoes are found where the Earth's crust is thin.

Volcanoes can also occur where the Earth's plates meet.

B

Our World

Mountains

By Sarah Levete

Aladdin/Watts
London • Sydney

© Aladdin Books Ltd 2006

Designed and produced by
Aladdin Books Ltd
2/3 Fitzroy Mews
London W1T 6DF

First published in
Great Britain in 2006 by
Franklin Watts
96 Leonard Street
London EC2A 4XD

A catalogue record for this
book is available from the
British Library.

ISBN 0 7496 6263 8

Printed in Malaysia

Editor:
Katie Harker

Design:
Flick, Book Design and Graphics

Picture researcher:
Alexa Brown

Illustrators:
Mike Saunders, Ian Thompson

Literacy consultant:
Jackie Holderness – former Senior
Lecturer in Primary Education,
Westminster Institute,
Oxford Brookes University

Questions, key words and glossary

Each spread ends with a question which parents and teachers can use to discuss and develop further ideas and concepts. Further questions are provided in a quiz on page 30. A reduced version of pages 30 and 31 is shown below. The illustrated 'Key words' section is provided as a revision tool, particularly for apprentice readers, in order to help with spelling, writing and guided reading as part of the literacy hour. The glossary is for more able or older readers. In addition to the glossary's role as a reference aid, it is also designed to reinforce new vocabulary and provide a tool for further discussion and revision. When glossary terms first appear in the text they are highlighted in bold.

 See how much you know!

Why do mountains form?

What are groups of mountains called?

Why do mountains look different?

Can you name the tallest mountain
a) on land?
b) under the sea?
c) on Mars?

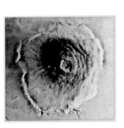

What do geologists do?

How do some animals adapt to mountain conditions?

What is the air like at the top of a mountain?

How is pollution affecting mountains?

Key words

Surface

A

Block	**Dome**
Fold	**Mountain**
Plateau	**Range**
Rock	**Valley**

Volcano

Glossary

Ash – Tiny pieces of lava.
Erosion – The effect of weather and glaciers wearing away hard rock.
Erupt – When magma bursts out of the Earth's crust.
Extinct – A volcano that will not erupt.
Fertile – Land that can grow plants easily.
Glacier – A huge river of ice that slowly moves down a mountain.
Lava – When magma bursts out of the Earth's surface, it is called lava.
Magma – Boiling sticky rock.
Plates – Huge rocky pieces that make up the Earth's outer surface.

B

Pollution – Gases, chemicals or rubbish that harm the natural world.
Terraces – Steps cut into the hillside for farming.
Tsunami – A very large ocean wave caused by an underwater earthquake or volcanic eruption.

What is a mountain?

The surface of the Earth is full of bumps, hills and valleys. We call the tallest places on Earth 'mountains'. Life in the mountains is cold and harsh but many people, plants and animals are able to live there.

▶ **Mountains come in all shapes and sizes.**

No two mountains look the same! Some are pointed and jagged. Others are rounder and smoother. There is no agreed definition about when a hill becomes a mountain, but generally mountains are more than 700 metres tall. Mount Everest is the tallest mountain on land and is 8,850 metres tall.

▶ Mountains are made from rock.

There are three main types of mountain rock, depending on where the mountain is found and how it formed. Granite is very hard and looks grainy, like a mixture of salt and pepper. Sandstone is made of squashed up grains of sand. Limestone is mostly made from the remains of dead plants and animals.

Limestone

Granite

Sandstone

Groups of mountains are called ranges.

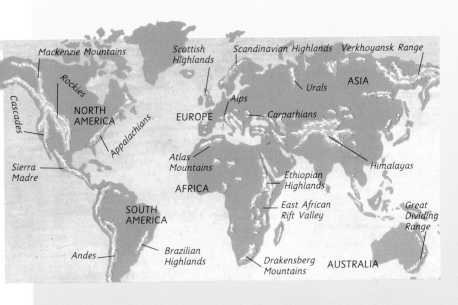

Mackenzie Mountains

Rockies

Cascades

NORTH AMERICA

Appalachians

Sierra Madre

Andes

SOUTH AMERICA

Brazilian Highlands

Scottish Highlands

Scandinavian Highlands

Verkhoyansk Range

ASIA

Urals

Alps

EUROPE

Carpathians

Atlas Mountains

AFRICA

Ethiopian Highlands

East African Rift Valley

Drakensberg Mountains

Himalayas

Great Dividing Range

AUSTRALIA

Most mountains are grouped together in ranges, such as the Alps in Europe and the Atlas mountains in Africa. The highest range of mountains in the world is the Himalayas range in Asia.

Which mountain range is the nearest to your home?

How mountains form

Mountains take millions of years to form. Huge movements deep in the centre of the Earth slowly push rocks into mountain shapes. Some mountains, like the Urals in Russia, started to form about 250 million years ago.

▲ The Earth's surface is like a rocky jigsaw.

The outer layer of the Earth is made from giant pieces of rock called **plates** which lie on top of boiling hot, runny rock called '**magma**'. The plates move about a thumb's length each year, but we can't feel them moving. When the plates push into or pull away from each other, rock is forced upwards forming a mountain. This aerial view shows a fault in Tibet in Asia. The Kunlun fault is 1,500 km long. It can be seen running from left to right. Lines of vegetation are shown in red.

◀ Some mountains are still growing!

Some plates that collided millions of years ago are still pushing together, and causing the land to rise upwards. The Himalayas in Asia grow about six centimetres each year. Soft soil above the Asian plate is rising because it is being pushed by the stronger Indian plate.

Geologists study mountain rocks.

Geologists are scientists. They study rock layers and the ways that rocks form. By examining rocks, they are able to work out how a mountain formed and even how old it is! Geologists use a range of tools, from hammers and chisels to drills, satellites and computer technology.

 How do we know how mountains form?

Mountain types

Different movements of the Earth's crust cause mountains to form. As the plates move together or apart, four main types of mountain are created – dome, plateau, block and fold mountains.

▶ **Dome mountains are rounded, while plateau mountains have flat tops.**

Dome mountains form when hot runny rock (magma) under the Earth pushes up and bulges out. Plateau mountains have steep slopes rising to a large area of flat land. They can form in different ways – when plates push together or magma is pushed to the surface.

(Above) The Putorana plateau, Siberia. Dome mountains of the Li River, China.

▶ The Sierra Nevada mountains in the USA are block mountains.

When the Earth's rocky plates pull apart, the outer surface of the Earth cracks. Massive chunks of rock collapse leaving blocks of mountains on either side. Block mountains have flatter peaks than fold mountains.

The Andes in South America are fold mountains.

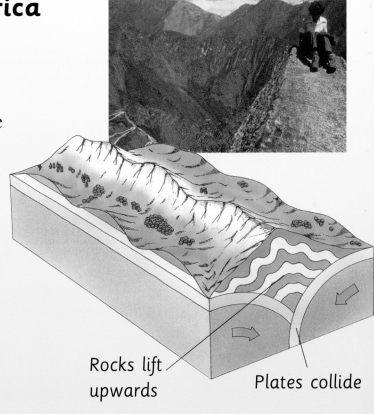

Fold mountains are formed when one plate bumps into another and keeps moving, causing layers of rock to crunch together and lift upwards. Fold mountains are mainly made from softer rocks, like limestone. The Himalayas in Asia and the Alps in Switzerland are also fold mountains.

Rocks lift upwards

Plates collide

 What can happen if the Earth's rocky plates move quickly?

Exploding mountains

Sometimes mountains are formed when boiling runny rock bursts from the ground and hardens. These mountains are called volcanoes. They can be made in a few days! Some explode without warning. Others will never explode again.

◄ Volcanoes are found where the Earth's crust is thin.

Volcanoes can also occur where the Earth's plates meet. When one plate slides under another, the magma on which it lies **erupts** out of the Earth. The magma is called **lava** when it comes to the surface. Liquid lava cools and hardens to form mountain rock.

► **Living near an active volcano is dangerous. They may explode at any time!**

Volcanoes often change shape – they can erupt suddenly or even collapse. In the 1980s, steam and ash unexpectedly erupted from Mount St Helens, USA. Some very old volcanoes are called dormant (or sleeping) volcanoes. Volcanoes that will never erupt again are called **extinct**.

When boiling hot rock is forced out of the Earth it can be thrown 600 metres into the sky!

Lava

Ash

Magma

When a volcano erupts, huge pieces of rock fly into the air and clouds of **ash** smother the land around. The suffocating ash or red hot lava can kill people. Volcanoes can also cause earthquakes, making the earth shake.

 What do you think it is like to live near a volcano?

Mountains everywhere

We see land mountains in many parts of the world. But mountains can also be found under the sea and even on other planets in space. Scientists and explorers use special equipment to study mountains everywhere.

▶ **Mountain ranges can be found in the ocean.**

Some ocean mountains are so huge that their tops form islands where people can live – Iceland is one example. Mauna Kea, in Hawaii, rises 10,200 metres from the bottom of the sea. It is the Earth's largest mountain, even though Mount Everest rises 8,850 metres above land. Sometimes, gaps in the ocean rocks cause gas to escape and the water to boil.

◀ This mountain is found on Mars.

Space scientists have been studying the surface of other planets. They have found enormous volcanic mountains on Mars, like Olympus Mons, its highest mountain. It is 22,860 metres tall – three times higher than Mount Everest.

Special robots and cameras are used to study sea and space mountains.

Remote-controlled machines fitted with cameras travel millions of kilometres to Mars. They take pictures of the planet's mountainous surface. Underwater robots, called submersibles, look at the ocean floor and find out more about underwater mountains.

 Does the Moon have mountains? How do we know?

Shaping mountains

Most mountains are very old. But mountains like the Himalayas and the Rockies are young (only about 70 million years old!) These mountains have jagged peaks. Old mountains are smoother because their edges have been worn away.

▶ **Over thousands of years, rain, wind and ice wear away the hard rock.**

The effect of wind, rain and ice on the rock is called **erosion**. Rainwater seeps inside the rock and freezes. As it does so, the water expands and eventually cracks and breaks the rock. Fierce winds also blow sand and tiny pieces of rock onto the mountain, slowly wearing it away.

◀ Some mountain rivers are always frozen.

Rivers flow down mountains, carrying rocks and pebbles that cut into the rock. Up high, the rivers are frozen. These massive ice blocks are called **glaciers**. When glaciers move they crack the rock, and stones tear the mountain-sides.

Water carves out valleys as it flows down mountains to the sea.

Valleys are deep areas of land running between mountains. They are formed by the action of rivers and glaciers. Block mountains also create rift valleys (such as the Great Rift Valley in Africa) when the Earth's plates move apart. Valleys are very **fertile** because minerals in the river water are deposited on the flat land.

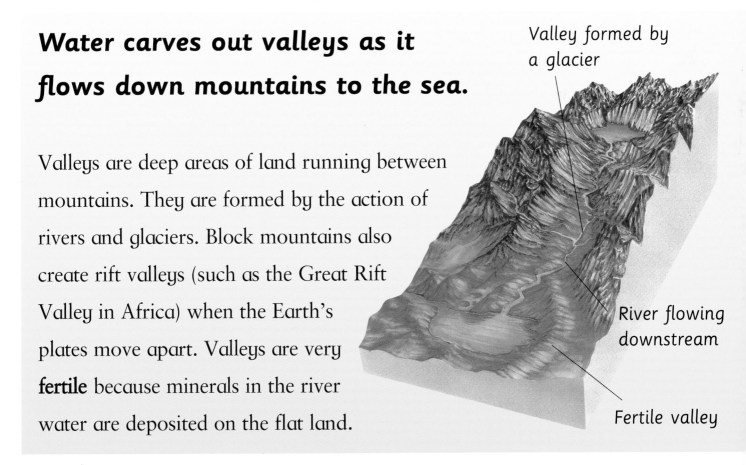

Valley formed by a glacier

River flowing downstream

Fertile valley

Why does water always flow towards the sea?

Weather up high

Mountains can be found in hot and cold countries. But if you go for a walk in the mountains, be prepared for any type of weather. Mountains can be sunny one moment, and cold and windy the next.

▶ There can be snow on mountain peaks in hot weather.

The highest part of a mountain is also the coldest. High up, the air is very thin and cannot hold much heat. Mountains are so tall that they make their own weather. They act as a barrier, forcing air to rise up and over them. The air cools when it passes over the mountain and this creates more rain and snow.

◀ Mountains can be wet on one side, but dry and sunny on the other!

The side of a mountain facing the wind is the wettest. This is because the wind carries warm, damp air that falls as rain when it reaches the cold mountain. By the time the air has passed over the mountain peak, it is drier and there is no rain left to fall on the other side! The dry side is said to be in a 'rain shadow'.

The mountains are getting warmer.

The chemicals and fuels that we use each day release harmful gases. This **pollution** traps hot air around the Earth causing temperatures to rise. As the glaciers melt, plants and animals move up the mountain, taking over from wildlife that used to live in colder parts. The land below may also flood.

 What kind of clothes should people wear in the mountains?

Mountain plants

Most plants need sunshine and warmth. On the low warm slopes of a mountain, you can see colourful flowers and trees. But on the icy peaks, there may be only a few tiny plants sheltering in rocky crags.

◀ **Most trees cannot grow high up in the mountains, but pine trees can.**

You will never see a tree growing on the top of a mountain – it is too windy and cold there! However, hardy, coniferous trees such as spruce fir and pine trees can survive the freezing weather of the higher slopes. Their tough bark protects them from the cold and falling snow does not break their branches.

▶ High up a mountain only small plants can survive.

Plants adapt to the harsh mountain conditions. Strong roots and short stems stop the fierce winds blowing them away. Small mosses cling closely to the rocks. Many plants also have small hairs to protect them from the cold.

As you move up a mountain slope you will find different trees and plants.

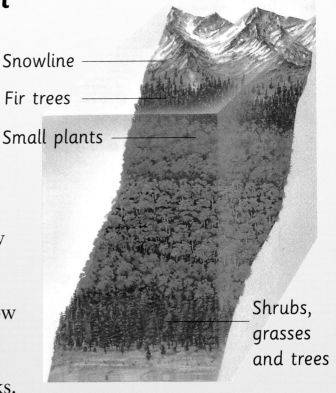

Snowline

Fir trees

Small plants

In the warm foothills, thick forests of broad-leaved trees soak up the sunshine. Further up, shrubs, grasses and trees grow and above this colder meadows of small plants and grasses are found. Fir trees grow further up the mountain. But beyond this there are hardly any plants in the icy peaks.

Shrubs, grasses and trees

 Why don't trees grow at the top of the mountain?

Mountain wildlife

The mountains are home to many unusual animals – from small hares looking for food on the rocky slopes, to large birds circling the craggy peaks. These animals have adapted to make the most of the cold mountain weather.

This snow leopard has a thick winter coat.

Snow leopards hunt in the lower mountain slopes, but in the winter they travel up the mountain to find more food. They need a thick winter coat to keep them warm. Mountain hares have a grey or black coat in summer but this turns white in winter to act as camouflage in the snow. Hares also have a thicker coat in the winter.

◀ Mountain birds use the wind to help them to fly.

Strong winds blow in the mountains. This golden eagle uses currents of air to fly. Eagles swoop down to pick up small mammals, such as rabbits and rodents. They have very good vision and can see prey up to three kilometres away! Other mountain birds, like the wallcreeper, peck at any insects they can find in the rocky crags.

Mountain goats have special hoofs to grip the rocks.

Mountain goats can move along narrow ridges, trotting away from hungry hunters. Their soft hoof pads are surrounded by hard sharp edges which help them grasp the rocks of steep mountain slopes.

 What other difficulties do mountain animals face?

Mountain people

About half a billion people live in the world's mountains. They have adapted to the bleak mountain conditions. Mountain people cut fields into the steep slopes to farm the land. They also use mountain animals for food, clothes and as a form of transport.

◀ **Some mountain people live in remote areas.**

Mountain people often live off what they can grow and farm. Sheep, goats, alpacas and llamas provide them with milk and meat for food, and wool and leather for clothes. Mountain animals are sure-footed and can carry heavy loads (or even people!) Although the air is thin, mountain people are able to travel in the mountains with ease. They can walk long distances and are confident climbers.

◀ **Tough crops such as tea, coffee and rice can be grown on steps cut into the steep slopes.**

Terraces are steps dug into the hillside. These steps stop soil and crops from being washed away by heavy rainfall. On the lowest slopes in valleys, the land is rich and fertile, and farmers are able to grow many crops easily.

More people now have easy access to the mountains.

Mountains were once used as a defence barrier against warring tribes. Now, many people have access to the mountains. Zig-zag roads and paths, cable cars and even train lines have been built up mountain-sides. Mountain tunnels allow vehicles to pass through. We can also access the mountains by air using helicopters.

 What are the advantages of living in the mountains?

Mountain treasures

Mountains provide us with many useful things – from metals deep in the rocky ground to fresh flowing mountain rivers. Mountains are also areas of great beauty and have become popular tourist destinations.

◀ Fresh water comes from mountain rivers.

All the major rivers in the world start as tiny streams and rivers running down mountain slopes. The great Amazon River in South America is fed by small streams from the Andes mountains in Peru and Bolivia. We use this fresh water to drink and to grow our food. The power of mountain rivers can also be used to make electricity.

Metals and jewels come from inside mountain rocks.

Many precious metals are found in mountain rocks. Most metals have to be mined, but some can be washed by the rain into rivers. Precious jewels, such as emeralds, are also mined from mountain rocks.

You can walk, climb or ski down a mountain.

Mountains have become popular tourist destinations because of their natural beauty. They are used for many sports, such as skiing, paragliding, walking and climbing. Some experienced climbers attempt to climb the highest peaks with the use of special training and equipment. In winter, many mountains become ski resorts when they are covered in snow.

Which famous mountain climbers can you name?

The future

The more we use mountains, the more we threaten the lives of the people, animals and plants that live there. We must continue to take care of our mountains so that they can be enjoyed by future generations.

◀ **Sometimes waste is stored inside a mountain.**

Some people think that mountains are a useful place to store rubbish because they are remote and scarcely populated. Tunnels can be made in a mountain to keep the rubbish out of sight. But poisons from this rubbish can seep into the ground, killing plants and animals that live nearby.

► The way of life in the mountains is under threat.

If levels of pollution increase and the Earth's temperatures continue to rise, life will get more difficult for mountain people. Food and fuel could become scarce as mountain habitats change. Melting glaciers are also likely to cause floods, soil erosion, falling rocks and landslides.

Mountains may change in your lifetime.

Over millions of years, mountains grow and mountains wear away. Sometimes, a natural disaster can change the landscape dramatically. In 2004, a **tsunami** was caused by an earthquake under the sea in Asia. Whole islands disappeared from view and many people drowned. We cannot predict how mountains will change. However, we can do our best to protect them.

 How can we help to protect our mountains?

See how much you know!

Why do mountains form?

What are groups of mountains called?

Why do mountains look different?

Can you name the tallest mountain

a) on land?

b) under the sea?

c) on Mars?

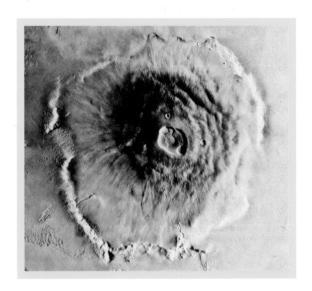

What do geologists do?

How do some animals adapt to mountain conditions?

What is the air like at the top of a mountain?

How is pollution affecting mountains?

Key words

Surface

Block   **Dome**

Fold   **Mountain**

Plateau   **Range**

Rock   **Valley**

Volcano

Glossary

Ash – Tiny pieces of lava.

Erosion – The effect of weather and glaciers wearing away hard rock.

Erupt – When magma bursts out of the Earth's crust.

Extinct – A volcano that will not erupt.

Fertile – Land that can grow plants easily.

Glacier – A huge river of ice that slowly moves down a mountain.

Lava – When magma bursts out of the Earth's surface, it is called lava.

Magma – Boiling sticky rock.

Plates – Huge rocky pieces that make up the Earth's outer surface.

Pollution – Gases, chemicals or rubbish that harm the natural world.

Terraces – Steps cut into the hillside for farming.

Tsunami – A very large ocean wave caused by an underwater earthquake or volcanic eruption.

Index